MW01027341

Me, mySelf

&

Dion Fortune

Alan Richardson

Self-published by the author
through Create Space
as he doesn't feel that this
enormously self-indulgent
if hugely proud-of-being-a-weird-kid
reminiscence
should waste a proper publisher's time and
money.

I have often said that it would take a book in itself to describe the incredible levels of chance, coincidence, synchronicity and totally bizarre serendipity that enabled (and often forced) me to research and write about this energy/entity/great magical soul known as Dion Fortune.
    This is the book.

Dedicated to:

Janine Chapman, Charles Fielding
Gareth Knight, Christine Hartley

&

Pat, Alexander and Jackie

&

Holly Ricciopo

&

(bestest of all)
Margaret Haffenden

We're all in this together

alric@blueyonder.co.uk
or
www.alric.pwp.blueyonder.co.uk

Penry and Violet

The Continuations of Dion Fortune

Today is October 5th 2015. As I scribble this on the right-hand side of a narrow-lined A4 notebook, sitting in the farm-shop caff on Winsley Hill, I can tell you with some confidence that it's exactly 48 years, 5 months and 6 days since I first heard the name Dion Fortune. I know that because I mentioned it in my tiny Silvine School Diary for 1967. I'm putting this all down now using a fine-tipped black ink pen which expresses, I think, the seriousness of my project. It also makes it difficult for anyone peering over my shoulder to see exactly what I'm writing about so earnestly. There is still a side of me which holds to the injunction that Eliphas Levi gave to would-be magicians over a century ago: To Know, Will, Dare, and above all Be Silent.

But two things are troubling me at this moment:

First, I promised my wife who is away in Gomorrah (aka Brussels) at the moment, that I would order a healthy lunch to provide all things necessary to help lower my blood pressure. Instead I await the arrival of a magnificent Bacon, Lettuce and Tomato sandwich with a side-order of fries. And I don't want her to find out.

Second, in those years since I first started writing about Dion Fortune I have altered my views of her several times - though not hugely.

So I'm wary about going over old ground as I want to keep this book to a series of simple yarns about how she impacted on my life.

When the first edition of *Priestess* came out via Aquarian Press I moaned about the fact that the current Warden of Dion's " Society of the Inner Light refused me access to their archives. I felt at the time that the published book was clunky, clumsy, derivative and a bit of a mess. To be fair to myself, though, I did the whole thing on an advance of £250 (pitiful even for those times), while working over 60 hours a week, living in a one-up and one-down rented cottage with my new wife and new first baby. Still, I hoped it would make me lots of dosh but in the event it cost me more to research than it ever earned in royalties. People didn't believe that but it's true.

Looking back now, some 30 years later I am thankful that the Warden (I think it was John Makin) was so un-cooperative. I just would not have understood the depths and subtleties of information their archives contained. Later, it was Gareth Knight, an initiate of the SIL and a formidable magus in his own right and rite, who made full and beautiful use of his unfettered access to those files and documents I had only dreamt about. His biography *Dion Fortune and the Inner Light* is the best one for any newcomers and the book I most envy.

However by the time I came to do the second version of *Priestess* for Thoth

Publications I had become aware that I was being influenced by young Violet Firth and Mrs Violet Evans more than that extraordinary magical being I might call DNF.

Magicians out there will know what I mean by that. If you're new, then bear with me as I come to explain.

By the time I came to write - or was compelled from inner sources to write - *Aleister Crowley and Dion Fortune*, I was seeing her and the Beast from a slightly different angle. Though I don't need to go into detail about that aspect here.

But now... gosh, the BLT cometh, radiating bliss, brought into the room by a comely maiden as if she were carrying the Dodgy Dish that some call the Holy Grail.

It's not Pentecost is it?

I'll come back to you all soon...

*

It was in Herman Hesse's classic *Demian* that a character thundered:*No-one hears about Abraxas by accident, make a note of that! I'll tell you even more about him. I know a little about him...*

I tried to read that book as a teenager but never got the end. I can't recall now whether it was too intellectual for me or just plain boring in comparison with those Science Fiction novels by Isaac Asimov, Ray Bradbury and Robert Heinlein which romped me across the antic galaxies of infinite space. But those words stuck in my mind even though the rest of Demian's world sank like Atlantis.

Perhaps my own daemon decided that when I read that sentence I had no need for the rest of the book. Although I won't thunder at you, I think the same is true of Dion Fortune. She never comes to you by accident. I know a little bit about her. If I tell the story about me and her it is not to claim any degree of singularity. My aim, simply, is to trigger the awareness that her energy, her magic, is in all of you too, in ways you might not be aware. Make a note of that.

Although I have stayed well away from recreational drugs and can't cope with anything stronger than a steaming mug of Tetley's tea, there is also something that Timothy Leary wrote which is crucial. After doing some heavy acid tripping with Brian Barritt at Bou Saada he realised that, at the same place but 50 years earlier, Aleister Crowley and Victor Neuberg had been doing much the same. Crowley's aim had been to rise up the inner dimensional realms of the 'Enochian Aires' that Dr Dee and Edward Kelly had named and explored in the Elizabethan era.

So Leary felt that he was a 'continuation' of Crowley, as opposed to a reincarnation; there were strong parallels between his and Barritt's experiences, and those of Crowley and Neuberg, and thus by extension Dee and Kelly. Leary saw himself as part of a line of sorcerers who recurred throughout history, and felt that he was playing out a kind of cosmic script for a regular transformative current that repeated itself throughout time.

Well, I suggest that we can also see ourselves as playing out our own cosmic scripts with regard to Dion Fortune and her peers. We are continuations, parts of a transformative current. If she has reincarnated at all (and I have met several thoroughly stable women who have claimed her as a previous life) then it is within our own psyches rather than bodily. She has bits and pieces inside our souls. Our whole life is a ritual drama. We start off as understudies but then we take on the main role. Where the notion of Free Will comes into it I really don't know. Perhaps if I'd read to the end of *Demian* I might have had some ideas about that.

Someone once wrote - actually I think it was me - that when you become aware of the Old Gods, they become aware of you. Old gods, older goddesses, Masters, faery beings, tree spirits... We are connected in myriad ways. A yarn springs to mind here, told me recently by a highly experienced magician who was doing some advanced group work in a little house in Glastonbury.There was a simple mirror on the wall. Beyond that wall, the house adjoining was where Dion had lived. During the rite he had the uncanny perception of seeing that lady herself, peering out from the mirror at them as if it were a window. Before the next piece of magic the magus of the group, without any comment, covered up the mirror.

In some ways we are all participants in the work she did up until her death in 1946. Today, she can also take part in the stuff *we* attempt and will often peek in to see what we get up to. Later in this book I'll talk about the very strange time when I typed up the Magical Diaries of two senior figures within her group and felt - knew - that in some odd ways I was involved in rites that had been worked in her lodge 50 years before.

*

I am sitting scribbling now in the driver's seat of the specialist Mobile Library that I manage for

the Council. It is the best job I've ever had. I

visit the elderly in remote homes and isolated communities across my magical county of Wiltshire.Today I'm on Route D which means I start at Sutton Veny then wend my way toward Tisbury.

Tisbury is a gem of a town but I often break out into a sweat and invoke all sorts of deities when taking my large 7.5 tonne vehicle down the very narrow and very steep high street hoping that nothing comes the other way. Still, in the sheltered accommodation for the elderly at the bottom, I have some voracious readers of Large Print Thrillers.

Most of my readers throughout the county are women because they live longer than us men. They nearly all love a good Murder, as they call it. Preferably British. As foul as I can provide. They've no interest in my vast selection of Large Print Romances; they've been there and done all that in their lives.

I drive through the huge arch at the entrance of Fonthill Park and stop for a moment to salute the Green Man (or is it an imp?) which forms the keystone on both sides. Then marvel at the utter beauty of this area. This was the domain (or do I mean demesne?) of that mad bugger William Beckford. I keep getting nudged to write a mad book about him some day but I know that won't happen.

I've got plenty of time before Tisbury so I stop for a moment in the lay-by next to lake. I have healthy packed sarnies made by Margaret.

They are composed of slices of rye bread packed with hummus, rocket, cherry tomatoes and sprinkled with toasted pumpkin seeds. I'm sure they will be delicious, but I'll start with what the people in Gomorrah would describe as an *amuse-bouche* and attack my hidden cache of Kit-Kats first.

Nordic walkers come past. They give me rictus grins but don't pause. Everyone smiles at the Mobile Library. I smile back and wave, but I do think that men should be banned from wearing spandex.

Ahead of me, at the junction next to the Beckford Arms, is a signpost. I know the route intimately now and don't need the information it supplies. But it makes me think.

As I look back toward Dion's first arrival in my life, I must summon up the image of a signpost. We all have some of these in our psyches. In my mind's eye they are old black and  white posts taller than myself, rising from a grassy crossroad, with arrowed boards sprouting out which give clear directions and often several choices of travel. Sometimes they give information telling you the distance to the next stop; or point out where you have just been and how far you have come. The measurements on them are not in miles but in years. They are not always comfortable places to linger but they enable you to pin certain moments in your mind so that you mutter to yourself: *I remember, I remember...* and evoke things lost or well avoided.

There is a beautifully melancholic poem by Thomas Hood[1] that everyone should track down. In it he entwines his innocent heaven-touched childhood with his own wistful and perhaps mournful present in a way that we can all say: *I've been there too.* The final three lines are:

> But now 'tis little joy
> To know I'm farther off from heav'n
> Than when I was a boy.

He died quite young, but not before he crafted serious and quite excellent poetry about Fairies and Centaurs from his sick-bed. Whenever I first read that poem I thought of Dion Fortune's comment in her *Esoteric Orders and their Work:* "The 'heavenly homesick' are many, but those who will endure the divine journey are few." I'm pretty sure she liked Hood's poem too, and knew exactly what he meant. Perhaps all of us 'continuations' reading this, who have not stumbled upon her Abraxian name by accident,

---

[1] 1799-1845. Full poem in Appendix A

have always been inspired and cursed in equal measure by this same homesickness.

So I remember - I do so *clearly* remember, honest! - a moment before my birth in which the formless entity known as 'I' seemed to look down and choose the young couple who would be my parents. Was her essence up there with me in-between the lives? I have no sense of that. But I do think that my first marker was created then. If I were to give such an elusive moment and such an astral signpost a tenuous shape then its single arrowed board would bear the single and rather scary word GO!

Those parents of mine, who influenced me in murderously loving ways but to whom I was never conversationally close, must themselves have had a whole host of signposts in their own lives. They were of the generation who would - although they never did to me - reminisce about where they were and what they were doing when they heard that the War had ended, or of the death of King George VI shortly after I was born. Though I don't think was responsible for *that* one.

Years later this sort of thing became part of the folklore which held that everyone can remember where they were and what they were doing when they heard of President Kennedy's assassination. Even now, several generations at once can close their eyes and zoom back in Time and Space to that marker and evoke frozen instants of worlds that have long since gone.

As I write this, in 2015, Kennedy's role has been taken over by John Lennon, Elvis Presley, Princess Diana and someone called Kurt Cobain. There's a biography about him in the back of my Van but I've no intention of reading it. Plus I imagine there's a host of others completely unknown to me who have taken on these mantles for the generations to come. Goodness knows who will hammer in such dread posts in the time-lines of my grand-children.

I have written elsewhere in my tongue-in-cheek autobiography *The Google Tantra - How I became the First Geordie to Raise the Kundalini*[1] of how it was actually that long-gone rascal-guru 'Lobsang Rampa' who drew me toward a path I have never since left, although I've changed direction a few times.

No-one reads him now. He never quite got over being exposed as Cyril Hoskins from Thames Ditton in Surrey. I won't have a word said against him.

During my teens years in the old coal-mining town of Ashington, in Northumberland, I had a self-imposed habit of going 'up the street' as we called it, every Saturday morning. As I sit here in one the

---

[1] New edition entitled *Sex and Light - How to Google your way to God-hood.* Twin Eagles Press.

prettiest places in the south-west of   England, keeping and eye on the time as I dwell on timeless memories, I can look down upon this youth.

I suppose I'm an echo (perhaps another sort of continuation) of that formless, shining, pre-incarnation that was 'I', imbued with some thin awareness of how it would all work out.

Come up next to me and see...

It is 1965 so I'm almost 14. I'm on a street in the town of Ashington, in Northumberland. It is sunny and cold. The street in question is Woodhorn Road which melts into Station Road where the main shops are, running rigidly from east to west. I'm dawdling along on the southern side, heading westward as far as I can go. Along the way I pop into John Baker's Shop to see if any new Airfix or Revell model aeroplanes have arrived, of which I already have a couple of dozen in my bedroom, deftly assembled but never painted. Then up to Woolworth's to browse through the cheap paperbacks, looking for another by Arthur C. Clarke.

Last month I stumbled upon his collection of short stories called The Other Side of the Sky and am still thrumming from the idea that God might have nine billion names, all of which can be snuffed out in some quiet apocalypse; but mainly I'm gripped by the notion that other realms might exist beyond this one. Thanks to him and his peers I am no longer quite so interested in cowboys or getting to Dodge City. Now, I would far rather man an intergalactic Way Station like the solitary character in Clifford D. Simak's novel.

I am, I feel, growing up; my burgeoning bum-fluff moustache is proof of this. My friend Maxwell assured me yesterday that if I rub it with linseed oil as used on cricket bats, it will surge manfully. I continue past shops with odd names like Doggarts, Arrowsmiths, Boasts and Crisps, avoiding the rough lads that go to the numerous Secondary Modern schools who might regard me, a grammar school boy, as a mortal enemy and duff me up. When I get as far as the Regal Cinema I cross the road and return along the less-interesting shops on the northern side, heading eastward now...

It was while I was heading on this ritualistic  eastward path that I felt compelled to enter the rather run-down newsagents on that side and was drawn to the shelf containing a single copy of Lobsang Rampa's *You - Forever.* There was nothing spicy on the cover, not like those books which Maxwell had found when doing a routine search of his parents' drawers. Nothing to appeal to my exploding libido. Just that bland title and the picture of an old man's bearded face.

Yet it fell open of its own accord and there was a line drawing of a naked young woman and the astral body rising above her, connected by a silver cord, and it felt as though I had been hit by a hammer. I knew this. I had not - then - been out of my body or even heard the term astral projection but I just knew that this was real, and part of what I was looking for, and part of *me*.

This book (which I've still got) blasted open inner doors that caused me to become obsessed by Yogis and Yoginis, Arahats, Mahatmas, Devas, gurus, wonder-working lamas and numerous Himalayan Masters with names even more exotic than the shops in Ashington: Djwal Khul, Mingyar Dondup, Morya, Koot Hoomi lal Singh[1]. Everything Eastern came to obsess me. I stormed along the Noble Eightfold Path and worked toward its Four Noble Truths. I marvelled at Parahamsa Yogananda and observed how, in Hinduism, Krishna was seen as an avatar of Vishnu. I liked that word, avatar, and am pleased that it has entered common usage. I learned about the chakras and mudras, the ida, pingali and kundalini and how to sit in the lotus position - the padmasana - and practise the pranayamic breathing exercises that Lobsang taught me, aiming for *tummo,* raising my body

---

[1] Now sanitised as Kuthumi. I wonder why later writers were worried by the lal Singh?

temperature in the cold sitting room through mastery of my inner fire. I did get up a small sweat.

I hailed the jewel in the lotus, tried to read the akashic records and took in enough *prana* to float a Zeppelin. Then I learned about the different planes of existence and searched around in Secret India and Secret Egypt, and tried to understand the difficult concept of the Overself. Everything spiritual was Eastern, everything Eastern was spiritual. I yearned to have the mighty Koot Hoomi appear to me in the park in Ashington as he done to Madame Blavatsky in London.

Hedging my bets, I also looked for the Buddha everywhere. And Krishna, and Guru Nanak and Padmasambhava. I daydreamed in school about *pralaya*, or the Night of Brahma, when the entire universe would dissolve into blissful nothingness, to be followed eventually by the Mahamanvantaric dawn when it would all waken again and, hopefully, I would not have to do P.E. or double Metalwork ever again. But I did agonise how I would prepare my parents for all this and only only hoped that my voice would deepen and my moustache arrive before it all kicked off.

It was at this time that the invisible energy which I later called the Library Angel flapped itself into my life and wrapped rainbow wings of happenstance around me. Was it a splurt of energy from this Overself that Lobsang talked about? Maybe it was directed by Dion Fortune? Was she 'within' my Overself - part of it - so as I became aware of it, she (and a host of others in there) became aware of me? I don't know.

Throughout that small diary for that single year (which I've got in my top pocket now) I recorded my astral projections and terrified exploration of what was still called 'self-abuse'.

It took me years to realise that Dion had the same agonies. In fact in the years before the Great War she had made a living teaching people how to sublimate their desires. In my little diary I find sad entries which say: "I will never control this." And then another in which I had used a technique that might have been created by Dion herself in which I commented: "Practised my new meditation. Very pleasant. No desire to ♂ Perhaps I am cured? I AM cured!"

I was 15 in 1967, remember, and although I had not yet stumbled upon her, the door to Dion's era had not yet closed. I still believed the teachings of Alice Bailey, Charles Leadbeater, Lobsang, Annie Besant and a host of others who insisted that spirituality and sexuality were incompatible. They were mighty Adepts! They were on the verge of Nirvana! They could not be wrong, could they?

Thank the gods another door was opening and I found myself entering an era in which, as someone in a fillum said, 'Everything changed.'

And thank even more gods that I eventually stumbled upon Aleister Crowley, is all I can say...

*

I am parked up now opposite Silbury Hill and re-reading what I've typed up so far. Thanks to the computer terminal behind the driver's seat I can access the internet and all my old manuscripts on my flash-drive. The library software which enables me to issue, discharge, make reservations etc. is known as Galaxy. I tell my fellow librarians that I'm a Master of the Galaxy but they beg to differ coz they know my stock is all awry and my admin is a complete mess.

Although I always say hello to King Zel who is said to inhabit Silbury, I have no sense of presence. Instead I sit for a moment and brood and reminiscence, sometimes scribbling into my notebook, sometimes directly onto the pc, emailing it to myself to work on properly, later.

I have just come from Marlborough. Merlin's Borough. Only one caff of any charm. My readers there are wonderful - real role models for when I grow up - but I don't like the town although it's pretty enough.   If it was a woman you would describe her as having fur coat and no knickers. People from Ashington will know exactly what I mean by that.

The Chippenham Mobile Library driven by Ron thunders by, beeping loudly. It is bigger than mine, and caters for children also. His

Large Print section is pitiful. There are some people climbing Silbury despite the clear notices telling people not to. That annoys me. And I sit and think, and I sit and remember.

I shouldn't be lazy about this but I'm rather taken by this glorious computer programme just a click away called Google Earth which allows me to summon up Ashington as it is today and even gives me a little wobbly man that I can shake around and drop down into it - much like my soul in that pre-incarnationary moment in that astral realm that Lobsang might have called the *kama loka*.

If you were to do that yourself you'd see the newsagents is now a shiny Army Careers recruiting office. Directly opposite that, today, is Dukes shop which sells uniforms and workwear and kingsize clothing for men. In my day it sold plastic models, balsa kits, simple bits and pieces for DIY, and had one revolving rack for small digest-sized paperbacks that no-one else seemed interested in. It was here that I can hammer in a clear signpost; because one Saturday morning as I headed Westward on my ritual walk, I first saw the odd name 'Dion Fortune'.

It was a small American monthly magazine called 'Exploring the Unknown'. It impressed me enough that I made mention of buying it in my diary for the 29th April 1967: "Got Ex. T. U. At Snotty Johns. Played cards with Maxy this after. He beats me every time.'

As I flicked through to the last pages there

was a small Letters to the Editor section, and a flurry of discussion about this odd topic of psychic attack. I hadn't realised there was such a possibility! Far from being scared, I was thrilled. One of the correspondents wrote - and I remember his opening words exactly if the rest of it goes a bit wonky - "Now I regard Regardie (no pun) as my best friend, so to speak, but Dion Fortune's *Psychic Self Defence* is the best book on the topic."

I had no idea who this Regardie was but the instant I saw the name Dion Fortune I entered (not for the first time even then) into what I now think of as a 'bell-jar'. That is, a localised silence in which I was fully aware of the noises and activities around me: stillness, calm, peace, and a sense of not being quite in this world. I later came to hear others describe this feeling as the Oz factor, or perhaps even Castaneda's 'Stopping the World'.

'Dion Fortune'... what an odd name! A fella, obviously, as it summoned up an image of an American evangelist from the Deep South, with a crisp white suit and a weird toothy grin and lacquered bouffant hair.

I must have stood there for some time as the shop owner, whom I always knew as Snotty John, was looking warily at me as if might shove the magazine under the armpit of my jacket and walk out. During those days I learned that my armpit could conceal surprisingly large objects but I knew that, in some ways, I was on holy ground just then. I paid him 2/6d and walked on up the street, ever Westward from then on.

*

I hesitate to say that Me and Van are One but it certainly doesn't like it when anyone else drives it when they cover for me during holidays. When they do, the lift for the disabled doesn't work; the power doors refuse to open; Galaxy refuses to co-operate.

In a very real sense Dion Fortune was ultimately responsible for this job I have now, driving my still magnificent but falling-apart Van. This might seem a preposterous connection or chain of circumstance, but indulge me for a moment longer.

I realise now that this moment when I first saw her name was one of those events beyond Time and Space. My encounter with Dion Fortune's essence created a strange path for myself which took me deeper into the Mysteries yet was invisible to almost everyone else. It took me several decades before I became aware of a mass of pilgrim souls alongside me which took on shape and substance as we progressed. Our experiences might have been separated by years and distances, yet somehow they too shared that 'bell-jar moment' and came to make their invariably lonely progress through the 'normal' world while keeping such odd inner liaisons hidden from those around.

I am sure that whoever is reading this is now multi-tasking: taking on board whatever images my tale might summon up, while at the same time fully aware of their own personal first encounter. Like me they will have found that related material - books articles, chance conversations - would surge into their life with irresistible and bewildering force. Remember that this was an era when there was no instant access to information via the internet, no social networks.

Y'see in ways that the present generation might not easily appreciate, there was no great public interest or sympathy for such arcane topics in the mid-1960s. At least not in Ashington. If there was an 'anything goes' counter-culture and a supposed 'occult explosion' then, be sure that the shock waves didn't arrive there either until much later.

There was a moment on BBC when David Frost hosted some studio discussion and a member of the audience said they believed in reincarnation. Frost and the rest of the audience laughed, it was such a bold statement to make in those times and a bizarre belief to hold. How could I go to the local library and order anything with a title as lunatic as *Psychic Self Defence*?

So I learned early on to keep quiet about such things after I gained the mocking nickname at school of MahaRichy.

*

For me, at that time, this odd name 'Dion  Fortune' hung around at the front of my mind. As is the way with these things, I soon stumbled onto Richard Cavendish's thick and ominously entitled: *The Black Arts*, with the sort of cover that I would never dare let that all-powerful being known as The Mam see. I had no interest in the long first sections on witchcraft. I went straight into the index and there it was: *Fortune, Dion: 87, 161, 230, 257, 259.*

I remember trembling slightly, as if I'd been stalking someone and was now close to my prey yet with no clue what to do next. I pounced on the chapters entitled *The Cabala and the Names of Power* and the irresistible *Necromancy and Psychic Attack.*  I had no idea who or what this Cabala was and no clear understanding of Necromancy (I still don't) but I knew that the Eastern journeys of Young Alan were over.

It was on those pages that Cavendish actually quoted from that book with the extraordinary title: *Psychic Self Defence*. Here, it seemed, was real Magic that *anyone* could do. Here were real adventures unlike any that even dear old Lobsang had ever described. I no longer needed to go to Lhasa, or Benares because the marvels were happening here, in Britain. They could even happen amid the pit heaps of Ashington!

I just had to buy this book.

*

I think that when you find what might be termed your true path – however twee that might sound – you find yourself tested. Usually in proportion to your means. My 'means' worked out as follows: This wondrous book was all of £1/10/6 pence. My pocket-money was 2/6 pence a week (25 pence in today's money). Assuming that I spent none of my pocket money and saved every penny it would take me 13 weeks of discipline and self-denial before I could afford it.

Now some years before, I, who had never been to church in my life, had been so inspired by the self-sufficient robot in Anthony Boucher's SF story "The Quest for St Aquin" that I tried to become a saint. Thought it might please The Mam. However after one night and two days I sussed that sainthood was intimately tied up with being po-faced, boring and talking in soft monotones. I gave that up when Bonanza came on the telly, because the urbane and often saturnine Adam Cartwright was a far more appealing character than Aquin and probably faster with a Colt .45.

So I felt certain that this 'Dion Fortune' probably wouldn't ask me to spend 13 ascetic and saintly weeks without any spending money. I sent out my first message on the inner planes asking for help. My inspired method for sending out a message on the inner planes involved taking a deep breath, holding it, squeezing tight my anal sphincter and stomach muscles and then, as I exhaled, sending out a telepathic message detailing my needs.

I don't know where I got that from but it worked; over the years since and many more anxious pleas my sphincter and six-pack have developed enormous strength. Indeed, I once challenged Maxwell to punch me in the stomach just to confirm this but he kicked me in the knackers instead. Though you probably don't want to know that.

Out of the blue, then, I was offered a job as waiter on Saturday evenings, Sunday lunchtimes and Sunday evenings in the splendidly entitled "Hirst East End and District, Club and Institute Union affiliated, Working Men's Social Club". Known simply as the East End, it was just one of 27 other Working Men's Clubs in a town with a population of 25,000. The job itself didn't appeal to me one bit but I knew that this was a response from Above. Or rather from Within.

Today, there seems to be this thing called Cosmic Ordering whereby you are promised infinite riches just by adopting a particular Attitude. The runtish little celebrity Noel Edmunds claimed he just poked his head out of his car window and laid out what he wanted and it came to him. I've tried that too but it never worked. I feel strongly that in Magic you don't get owt for nowt. If I wanted the money for that book, I knew that I had to make an outer statement of inner intent and work for it. Something to do with exchanges of energy, and balancings.

So after my first weekend porting trays filled with pint glasses of Fed Special and Broon Ales (plus schooner glasses of lagers and limes for the pitmens' wives), in a long narrow room filled with the smoke of full-strength Woodbine and Capstans - everyone smoked everywhere in those days - I had enough dosh for what I wanted. Coughing slightly and stinking of beer, I then had to face a far sterner test... I had to use the phone.

As a culture we in Ashington were poor though we didn't know it. We never had hot water or indoor toilet or bath in our house until I was nearly 18. This was some ten years before the miners' strikes managed to win better wages for the workers. Though if you ask me it was still slave labour and the money was still never enough, and the miners all said they would nivver let their sons gaan doon the pits.

Very few people in Ashington owned cars. My dad never did, never learned to drive. Cars were so infrequent that the young bairns would sit on street corners and write down car number plates as today's 'anoraks' would do for trains. Phones were just unknown. The only phones that I knew of were in the red telephone kiosks which used the STD system. Today that acronym refers to sexually transmitted diseases and nothing else, but in the '60s it was Subscriber Trunk Dialling, a complicated system involving three buttons which you had to press in a certain sequence after feeding your money into a slot.

Phones were - and still are - something of a nightmare for me as I had a degree of unrealised hearing loss that was to cause endless problems over the years. Yet I took a deep breath, did that thing with my sphincter again, put my four large brown pennies into the machine and dialled Appleby's Bookshop in nearby (and posh) Morpeth. When the man answered I pressed button B as per directions. Trying hard to hide my embarrassment I asked in a high and nervous voice if he could order Psychic Self Defence by Dion Fortune.

Pardon, miss?

Psychic Self Defence by Dion Fortune.

The long silence, which ate up the money, was proof as to what a weird book it was.

What? By who?

I said it again. More silence.

Dae ye knaa the publisher, pet?

Aquarian Press.

Even more silence, then:

Aalright bonny lass. Shall ah send ye a postcard when it comes in?

Aye, ter A. Richardson, 59 Ariel Street, Ashington.

Then the money ran out and the line went dead and I gave a big sigh. I felt that I had passed a preliminary test, but also dreaded the next phase which might be called: Catchin' the Postie Before The Mam Saw...

*

I have written elsewhere about the fraught dynamics in my home[1]. I can't complain: that shining glob of pre-incarnationary consciousness I wrote about earlier clearly felt that this was the life I needed and the family I should choose. Now, decades later, I totally see it. I think The Mam became for me at that time a sort of Dweller on the Threshold whom I had to confront and get past, to realise that it was really aspects of myself that I was dealing with.

Now, I don't look back on her as this all-powerful destructive energy - a sort of Ashingtonian Kali - but as a scared young girl in a Mam's body, doing her best against things she couldn't understand. Which was ironic in that she once confessed her own Mam (whom I never met) had been 'fey'.

Nearly fifty years later and some 30 years after she died, I have a sense of Mam next to me. She is no longer a Dweller on the Threshold composed of all my quirks, fears and weaknesses.

---

[1] *Geordie's War*, Skylight Press

She is a young woman shaking her head at me. I close my eyes and listen:

> *So tell iz Alan... if ye knew that your teenage daughters wuz getting letters from complete strangers, and they wuz bein' secretive - how would ye feel? Would ye worry? Try to stop them?*
>
> *Ah jeezuz Mam of course Ah would. Ah see it noo. Ye were right. Ah'm sorry Mam... But doan't go on aboot it, eh?*

Prior to the start of my "DF Period" I learned what I had to do to hide the books that were coming into my possession from all sorts of directions. It was in this crucial year of 1964 that the weekly magazine " Reveille " had a half-page advert for *Bring Out the Magic in Your Mind* by one Al Koran. I suspected this was a pen-name. Without knowing, I  was already starting to learn the quality of Discrimination that kabbalists insist is the first Virtue on the path toward Godhood. The attraction for me was that the book (which cost £2) was offered on a ten days Free Trial. If the reader was not entirely delighted then he or she need simply return the book. Now I've never had much financial savvy, but it seemed to me that the company making the offer were mugs, or else supremely slow readers themselves; I knew I could devour it in an evening, copying by hand any nuggets it might contain.

When Koran's book finally arrived The Mam was horrified. You might have thought I'd summoned up the demon Choronzon from the Bottomless Pit. I think it was a combination of the price, and certainly the subject matter which caused this: her son wasn't normal. What would the neighbours think!? She went on and on at me. And on and on and on. And on. It was almost an ululation. I read it while she almost hovered over me, genuinely scared. There were no worthwhile nuggets inside. The guy was into what became known as Positive Thinking. Lobsang would have meant mincemeat of him - if he hadn't been a vegetarian.

But I learned from that time onward that if I wanted to bring such books into the house I would have to disguise them, usually by covering them in the brown paper jackets we had to make for all our school books, and put an appropriate hand-written title on the front to throw The Mam off the scent.

All these little challenges over the next couple of years prepared me for the moment when Appleby's postcard would arrive and the book would be awaiting which truly would bring out *real* magic in my mind, and none of this poncey stuff that Al Koran offered.

I broke the spring of the letterbox so that it would not snap shut and waited every morning for the postie to come. I had with me various brown envelopes which contained leaflets from aeroplane manufacturers such Hawker, Gloster, Vickers and Avro which had already sent me stuff for school projects. If she caught me waiting I could do a switch, easy peasy (This deception was a doddle; I still have the skills to make coins appear out of my grandchildren's ears.) The Mam didn't mind me obsessing about the Avro Vulcan V-bombers and their nuclear payloads and innovative Blue Steel stand-off missiles which could take out half of Moscow from 300 miles away: she just couldn't cope with spirits. Finally it came. Saturday morning. Hand-written in what I felt was a scornful manner. Psychic. Self. Defence. Waiting for me - little me! But addressed to Miss A Richardson.

The next challenge was the simplest. I had the exact money for the book but no extra for the bus-fare to Morpeth. Should I wait another week until I had enough? Absolutely not. I had some sense - I'm sure entirely imagined - that this Dion Fortune would approve of me walking there and back to show my dedication.

*

I'm in Salisbury now. I've got my notebook out again and am scribbling in the cafe of the Tesco Superstore. Last night Margaret made me a wonderful packed lunch with enough vitamins, minerals and other nutrients to help me grow into a big strong lad but I forgot to bring it. Often, when I've got what she calls Things in my Head, it's hard for me to remember the important things. So I've bought myself a Tesco's Meal Deal for £3.00 which includes crisps, a thin ham sarnie and a Diet Coke.

Sometimes I take my laptop to work with me to use during my break but I feel a bit twattish doing so.

I go to Salisbury every Wednesday, visiting half a dozen different homes each time. In fact during my monthly orbit I cover nearly 140 different places across the whole county, meeting all sorts of unusual folk. One was a friend of Om Sety; another a lover of Errol Flynn; various survivors of the Atlantic convoys during World War II (for whom I helped secure their recognition by the council); and more, many more. They are kind, and funny, but what gives me food for thought is that many of my newer readers in this service for the elderly are often younger than me.

Yet if I relax within the chaos my pen almost runs away with itself in a kind of automatic writing that was once the vogue among Spiritualists. A woman on the next table looks at me oddly. I'm sure she thinks that, from my intensity, I'm replying to a Dear John letter. I know that she has ordered something Vegan.

If only she knew my fascination as I time-travel to sink back into the teenager I was and summon up the excitement I felt on that day

when I went to buy Dion Fortune's awesome
book.

*

But excuse me if I pause a moment. Although
I've never delved further into the Akashic
Records than some accidental Remote Viewing,
I can sit here as an ageing man in the South West
of England and do some instant research into
those days when I was a young lad in the far
North East. To me the internet is just as good as
the fabled Halls of Akasha and far more reliable.
I know that, by using an on-line route-finder, the
distance between my old home in Ashington and
the bookshop in Morpeth is 6.9 miles each way.
I sometimes thought of myself as a bit of a
spacker as some called me in those days but I'm
now quite impressed. As for those who called
me this, I know that they're all bald, fat bastards
with a lifetime of tediums behind them and not
much ahead.

Now come up and join me between the
worlds again and look down to see how the next
part of the script plays itself out...

*Ah'm off ter see Maxwell! I lie to The Mam and
hope she doesn't notice that I'm going in the
wrong direction.*

*It's a warm day and the sun is at my back
as I head westward with my adolescent sense of*

Destiny pushing me. I am whippet-thin and freakishly fit. Like every young lad in those days I'm letting my hair cover my ears in homage to the Beatles and the Rolling Stones. I'm wearing

a white nylon shirt fastened at the collar, blue Maverick jeans and a light blue jacket which zips up the front. On my feet I've got a pair of desert boots which are all the rage then, but which are slightly too large for me. I belt along Woodhorn Road and on into Station Road, going faster than fairies, faster than witches, charging along like a trooper in battle. Or more pleasingly, like one of the tireless running lamas in Lobsang's Tibet[1].

I cruise through High Ashington and out along the road to Pegswood, with a vista of massive slag-heaps from the assorted collieries to my right and a hint of countryside to the left. Then down down the long road of the Whorral Bank into Morpeth which sits between seven hills like Rome. I am hot, sweating. I don't like the heat. But this is a test, I can't moan.

I go into the centre of the little town and turn up into Newgate Street. There is, truly, a new gate for me for go through at the end of it.

I give the man in the shop the much folded postcard.

It's for my sister I say, in a deep voice. He looks at me oddly. Does he recognise in me a nascent Master of the Occult as described by Richard Cavendish? Or just a bit of an eejit with more money than sense?

I try not to show my hands shaking as I put the book under my

---

[1] Oddly enough, although he never showed the slightest interest in my 'other' side, some 40 years later Maxwell confessed to me that around this time he was having powerful kundalini experiences. See Appendix 2 for his own inimitable descriptions of these.

armpit and walk out, dead casual, Alan-Head-in-the-Air.

I sit down on a patch of grass by the side of the road leading out of the town. Then take off the lurid cover and scrape off the title on the spine with a silver thruppeny-bit in case The Mam gets a glimpse of it before I can get it covered. I could have used an old brown penny but the silver rarity seems more fitting. As I do so I remember how Mam told me that two gypsy wimmen had come to our house in mid-winter 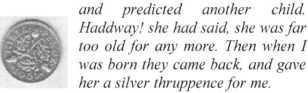 *and predicted another child. Haddway! she had said, she was far too old for any more. Then when I was born they came back, and gave her a silver thruppence for me.*

I open the book but am too excited to start at the beginning and make the normal progress. Words and phrases leap off the page as I dip into it at random. Passers by look at me oddly. I'm used to that. Fortune's text seems to glitter. I think I mean that literally. It might have been the Book of Kells. I have a sense of At Last! - as if I've glimpsed part of the machineries of the universe creaking into action. And, just before I close the book and make my sweaty way back home, I notice the sentence which tells me that she had studied at an occult college in the 'sandy fastness of the Hampshire Barrens.' I don't know why this leaps out at me before all the others but - Ye gods! - I yearn to know where that was! It had to be better than Ashington Grammar School!

I hadn't a clue where Hampshire was, much less those Barrens. I never dreamed that, very many years later, I would be the first person to track down the exact location of that college.

Appleby's Bookshop, meanwhile, has recently closed after 100 years but that patch of grass is still there, to the side of Dark Lane. I'll plant a signpost and won't care, now, if anyone looks oddly in that direction.

*

My last stop cancelled with a big sign on the door of the home saying D & V[1] so I've got a bit of time on the way back to base. I'm in a truck stop on the A36, some miles south of Warminster. It strikes me that I still have echoes of that defensiveness I had as a boy. Although I now have full and free access to a million books in the Wiltshire Library catalogue, I still order them in my wife's maiden name which she retains for her business. So that when they come through the loading bay to be sorted, the lads there won't think I'm a total nutter. The fact that I support and regularly flog that dead horse known as Newcastle United Football Club gives them no end of astonishment.

---

[1] Diarrhoea and Vomiting

So you'll appreciate that 50 years ago my Book of Books was quickly camouflaged and fitted nicely between school texts on History and French. I looked at it standing there, knowing that between those very ordinary 'O' Level texts was this one I had just bought, filled with paragraphs such as:

> I have had more than my full share of adventures on the Path; have known men and women who could indubitably be ranked as adepts; seen phenomena such as no seance room has ever known, and borne my share in it; taken part in psychic feuds, and stood my watch on the roster of the occult police force, which, under the Masters of the Great White Lodge, keeps guard over the nations, each according to its race; kept the occult vigil when one dare not sleep while the sun is below the horizon; and hung on desperately, matching my staying power against the attack until the moontides changed and the force of the onslaught blew itself out.

I had never read anything like it. I still haven't. Is it just me, or does anyone else hear the rhythms in which she often wrote? The stuff about defending yourself psychically interested me far less than the luminous and tantalising biographical details. If this was Magic then I wanted it, crazy, wild and hard - but not too scary! After all, it was not for nothing that Maxwell often called me Walter, Prince of Softies, after Dennis the Menace's enemy in the *Beano* comic. Him being Dennis of course.

Although it would enthral me, myself and I, to give full details of my exploding passion for what I now knew was the Western Mystery Tradition, this would drag on too long. In essence I stumbled upon second-hand copies of Dion Fortune's books in the most odd places and ridiculously unlikely ways. It was as though someone had placed Claymore anti-personnel mines along my path which exploded their shrapnels of knowledge right into my head. It was all entirely new and at the same time completely familiar.

There was one little tome in particular which did seem to call out to me. I was passing by the used book stall in the indoor Grainger Market (still my favourite place in the Holy City of Newcastle) when I glimpsed – or was drawn to – a little book in a crude orange cover which had the letters DNF stencilled on the front. Somehow I knew this was relevant although I had not yet learned that 'Dion Fortune' was a contraction of her family motto and Magical Name: Deo Non Fortuna.

The cover itself was made of that waterproof, thick, semi-plasticky material you used to cover kitchen tables with. You couldn't have peeled it off without destroying the whole thing. Those letters DNF...

I knew her real name was Violet M. Firth, no more than that, and felt rather shy knowing that much, as if I had compromised someone, come upon them unexpectedly. Yet when I picked up the book and opened it, I was somehow not surprised by the title: *Esoteric Orders and their Work*. This had clearly been sent to me.

But what did this 'N' stand for?

Plus that cover... Not as carefully cut and crafted as my own but far more durable. Perhaps there was someone else in Newcastle or around who also had to disguise such books from The Mam? Maybe I wasn't alone in my Quest? Maybe the person who covered this book was a young, slim lass with long dark hair and dark eyes and a pretty face! Someone who knew the different spellings of Kabbalah, knew what I meant by the words Sephiroth or Ain Soph Aur and had a great interest in taking off all her clothes and flinging herself at me!!

Alas as I browsed the delicious contents of my new find a middle-aged man appeared next to me, looked over at what I was reading, started making noises of interest and tried to draw me into conversation. I wondered for a second whether this was a mighty Adept making contact, but if so he wasn't even up to the Al Koran level of insight. It took me a couple of decades to realise that he must have been a paedophile, on the lookout for a vulnerable young boy like myself. Dion had warned about people like that in the other book. I mumbled excuses, paid for the book and left.

I don't know when I was able to make the connections which went:

Dion Fortune = Deo non Fortuna = Violet Mary Firth = Violet Mary Penry-Evans...

But I got there soon enough.

For a long time, however, I - like most others - assumed that Mrs Penry-Evans was a double-barrelled name. Instead she was using the convention, common for her generation, in which the wife would describe herself by her husband's name. So that my mother, for example, might have described herself as Mrs George Richardson, though she would rather have stuck needles in her eyes than actually do that.

It was a mistake which enabled Dion's magical superior Maiya Curtis Webb (later Maiya Tranchell Hayes) to hide from all modern researchers until, one feverish night working across the internet and Atlantic with William Breeze, the head of the O.T.O, we were able to track her down.

Though I'm not sure the spirit of Maiya has quite forgiven me for that.

Another story for another time, perhaps.

*

It is hammering down outside. I can hardly see to drive so I've pulled into a lay-by of the A4 along the road to Froxfield. My high van shakes and shrieks in the wind as if assailed by banshees. I rather hope that none of my readers have died, and that this is an omen. The rain bashes against the windscreen like the storm of reminiscence in my head and I'm aware that a mile beyond my final stop the dread spirits of the Berkshire Library Service hold sway.

I've found that driving, or being driven, induces in me a state of liminality: of being neither here nor there. I think that at these moments I'm - sometimes - in a state akin to walking za-zen. My mind is empty yet things come through, very gently.

There have been times in my long life when I have been so 'psychically thick' that it must have been a means to protect me. Or perhaps I was trying to protect myself from energies and entities which, while coming from supernal realms, showed moments of sheer stupidity. Believe what I say! There is a delicious yarn told me by the late and lovely Sue Kearley which I think is enormously important.

A very senior magician of her acquaintance - a Major Adept in fact - told her about his communion with an inner plane being who wanted him to do some work. The Magus pointed out that while he would like to co-operate, his life was quite difficult at that time in material and financial terms. He had bills to pay, a family to support, and not much money coming in to buy the time needed for such a mutual piece of Work.

So what do you suggest I do? The magician asked.

The being paused, thought, did the astral equivalent of stroking his beard and giving a hmmmm... and suggested:

Then find a King, and ask for gold...

Many times I've found myself at odds with what I might call my 'Inners' because they asked an awful lot of me without seeming to understand the sheer problems of life on earth. Many times I've had my own Rite Abuse to try and summon them up and give them a good slapping for their obtuseness. They forget, you see, the problems and torments of life in the material world. With some of them, they've never known.

Again, another story another time.

But there have been moments when I've been wracked by unexpected fevers, forced to take time off work, and have found myself plugged into Magical Currents that I could hardly resist, and *had* to bring them through with my writing.

At such times synchronicities came thick and fast - too many, too frequently, too complicated to detail here. And something of this sort was going on when, in 1968, the postie brought me the *New Dimensions Red Book* containing a photograph of Dion Fortune

I was too ill for school. My Dad brought up the package. I wasn't too worried about this because, with the title, I could claim it was a collection of Science Fiction short stories. I looked at the contents, which included: *Psychic and Occult Contacts; A Guide to Astral Magic; Four Magical Instruments* - oh and a long essay called *The Old Religion.*

What stunned me, almost shocked me out of my fever, was the first image of Dion. But what shook me even more was the immediate thought that - when the photo was taken - I was there. Somehow. In some way. Although I've learned since it was supposed to have been taken in Glastonbury I was quite certain this had been  taken - possibly by her father, in a London park.

I am not being coy. I simply report my first impressions and can't add more than that. I'd be quite happy to be proved completely wrong as to location. Whether I was there in a previous life (I doubt it), or there through a process of Remote Viewing (unlikely) I really cannot say.

*

Of course that single essay and method of self-initiation described in *The Old Religion* by the mysterious FPD had probably more impact upon me than Dion's stuff - which is saying something. I got to work on the techniques given in that essay at once, lying in my sick-bed trying to get to the Cave in the Mountains and the High Place of the Moon. I think I got there in the end.

If there is a signpost planted here then beyond it the road forks slightly, and two paths diverge into deep woods. Robert Frost's poem *The Road Not Taken* summons up something of my magical life from that moment, ending:

> Somewhere ages and ages hence:
> Two roads diverged in a wood, and I,
> I took the one less traveled by,
> And that has made all the difference.

As this is a book about me and Dion Fortune I don't really want to digress with equal details about this FPD. It took me another few years to learn that: FPD = Foy Pour Devoir = Kim Seymour; who was a very senior figure within Dion's magical lodge.

Besides, in working through Seymour's techniques while still convalescing from a high fever, it was another parallel with Dion' s youthful experience that inflicted me next. And thank god The Mam didn't see this one!

*

Y'see, even to my youthful, uncritical mind, there was some things in *Psychic Self Defence* that seemed pretty wacky.

Vampires, for one. She spoke in some detail about how some people are psychic vampires and I accepted that totally. Still do. I've met a few over the years who can drain energy from people and leave them feeling dirty. But she also spoke of the actual fangs-in-the-neck sort more usually seen in Hammer Horror Films. Even now, I don't know what to make of that and can only think that she was young when writing that book, and a little gullible.

And then there was a kind of Werewolf.

She had been hurt by someone whom she had tried to help, and was lying in bed resting one afternoon, deeply resentful and tempted to retaliate. As she brooded there came to her mind the thought that she should cast off all restraint and try going berserk:

> The ancient Nordic myths rose before me, and I thought of Fenris, the Wolf-horror of the North. Immediately I felt a curious drawing-out sensation from my solar plexus and there materialised beside me on the bed a large grey wolf. It

was a well materialised ectoplasmic form ... grey and colourless ... and it had weight. I could distinctly feel its back pressing against me as it lay beside me on the bed as a large dog might.

Although she knew nothing about the art of making Elementals at that time she had accidentally stumbled upon the right method - the brooding highly charged with emotion, the invocation of the appropriate natural force, and the condition between sleeping and waking in which the etheric double readily extrudes itself.

Well, I don't know about actual vampires (and I'm bewildered by the current obsession with these among the youth of today) but I fully accept her story about Fenris. It was about that time I created a Were-woman.

As I described it briefly in the first edition of *Priestess,* a similar thing happened to me. I was virgin, intense, pent-up with my adolescent energies and soaked with the atmospheres of magic that I was obsessing with, I came-to one morning after some fevered half-sleep and found a grey, cold, lifeless female figure next to me. It never stirred, the eyes never opened.

I peeked under the covers. The body was hairless but as shapely as a young lad would have wanted in his pervy fantasies. Remembering how Dion had dealt with Fenris, I drew it back inside me in case The Mam appeared and had a heart attack.

Just a dream? No. I've only recently read the psychologist Stan Gooch's book *The Origins of Psychic Phenomena* in which he described the succubus which appeared in his bed and had (entirely satisfactory) sex with him. It was a composite of various girls he had once known but with other elements not drawn from his memories in any sense. In my case it was the spitting image of a girl I was to meet in my second year at college. I didn't dare tell her that we'd already met, some six years before.

Again, I have no explanation for this. I only tell you what happened.

*

I knew from the book-jackets that Dion Fortune had died in 1946 aged 55, and that the lodge she formed still functioned. So of course I wrote to the Society of the Inner Light, as it was called, asking to join. As I recall, it was the Warden John Makin who replied telling me that I was far too young. I wrote a couple of more times after that, trying to wheedle information out of them, including asking for biographical details about the woman.

Makin's response to the latter was that the personality was not important: it was her teachings that mattered.

Even then, I disagreed. Still do. If it had not been for the luminous and compelling personality that came through in all of her writings, the SIL would have died with her. By having a literal bonfire of all such personal details (as I found out much later), and refusing to engage in the sort of speculations that came to obsess me, they actually created a cult.

Although I never met him I did come to learn one thing about John Makin which endeared him to me from afar. The man who managed his local library, Peter Larkworthy, was something a subtly influential figure in the shadows of the Wiccan movement. He knew exactly who Makin was, although the latter had no idea of what lay behind the young man stamping his books: all of which were Westerns.

As to this idea of Personality not being important...

I slowly became aware that I was more interested in Violet Firth than 'Dion Fortune'. And as time went on it was clear that she was quite happy to push me into certain areas involving her family background but kept me away from the arcane stuff which I couldn't have done justice toward.

*

I've long since learned that the crucial signposts in life are often so subtle as to be almost invisible - except in retrospect. This next one, perhaps more than any of the others, took me a little step closer to that woman who used the pen-name Dion Fortune.

As I have described elsewhere, in my *Letters of Light*,[1] I was 17 when I started to write to the magician William G. Gray in Cheltenham, going through the whole rigmarole of hiding his correspondence as before. How they managed to survive I don't know, as The Mam 'accidentally' destroyed a number of other letters which didn't evade her scrutiny.

When I finished at teacher-training college in Newcastle I applied for and got my first teaching job at Saintbridge School, Gloucester, just a few miles from Gray's place. I never wanted to teach. I wanted to write Timeless Prose and be near a *real* magician and learn the *real* stuff from someone who had known both Crowley and Dion Fortune and had worked magic with all those witches who had effectively invented their ancient Craft..[2]

The inner and outer events of this year are told in the little book mentioned above. The human side of the story is that it was one of the worst years of my life. But it was in the staff room one morning, during a break, that one of the other teachers, a certain Mr Wilby[3], mentioned a town not far away called Bath. He said it was beautiful. Said he'd love to live there.

---

[1] *Letters of Light,* Skylight Press 2015
[2] *The Old Sod,* with Marcus Claridge, Skylight Press
[3] No relation to Basil Wilby, aka Gareth Knight

It shows how parochial I was that I'd never heard of the place, but something nudged at me. Perhaps I just wanted somewhere beautiful, somewhere that didn't have hordes of pupils tearing me apart for being too soft. I took a sickie the next day, pretending my Dad had been injured down the pit and had to to go back up North for three days.

As W.E. Butler, whom I was also corresponding with and whose books I had also devoured once wrote: "A lie is an abomination in the sight of God, but a very real help in times of trouble."

Come upstairs again and look down:

It is May 1974. I have long hair and am wearing a denim jacket, blue and white hooped rugby shirt, blue flares and Green Flash trainers. I know, now, that the torments of the previous year are coming to an end and that I will be off to America soon on a phoney scholarship to the University of Kentucky.

The bus from Gloucester stops in what I imagine  *is the centre of this town called Bath. I get off next to Pulteney Weir and fall in instantly in love. I know that somehow, in the near future, I will come and live here.*

I go into the Parade Gardens which edge the river, sit on the grass and read the horoscope which Bill Gray's wife Bobbie did for me for the next year - without understanding any of it. It doesn't matter. I know that something in this place has drawn me here, and is silently communing with me. I just need to find a way of listening to the words.

I didn't know that, a century earlier, 'something' in the place had drawn and was communing with the parents and grandparents of Dion Fortune too.

*

I had various startling synchronicities involving Dion Fortune during my next years in the States but my complex and unhappy time there is not really part of this story.

As I always knew would happen, through a set of bizarre circumstances my first wife Cecilia was offered the post of Senior Dietician at the Royal United Hospital in Bath. I sort of bullied her, in a gentle way, into applying for it. Although she failed the interview and, upset, she wanted to go back to the States, I just KNEW that she would get a phone call. Two days later she got the phone call. The other successful applicant had unexpectedly withdrawn. Did she now want the job? We moved there from London in 1976.

But the next major signpost rammed into in my time-line was when, sometime in 1978, I got a letter inviting me to an interview. This was for a job as a senior teacher in a residential school in the village of Winsley, a few miles south of Bath. The school catered for what was then termed 'maladjusted' boys. That is, boys whose behaviour was so extreme that no ordinary school could cope. There were a lot of such places around at that time, and several in that immediate area. It was big money. Dreadful places, all of them.

I had no memory of even applying for the job and never wanted to go back into teaching. In fact I was quite happy working as a lowly-paid nursing auxiliary in Rock Hall House (formerly the Magdalen Hospital School) in Bath.

This was an old, rambling, delightful residential home on the edge of Combe Down, with views over to Westbury White Horse, catering for very young children with what are now known as learning disabilities: in those days they were mentally handicapped. I fell in love with most of them, seeing some of them at least as faery souls having their first go in our dimension. But as the home was likely to close, I went along to the interview in my best (only) suit.

*

There was only one other candidate there. Now pay attention folks because this is important, though it might take a while for me to explain why.

He had stayed in a Bed and Breakfast in Winsley village the night before. Like me the guy didn't seem interested in the job; like me he had no memory of even applying for it. We both must have done so months earlier, else how else could we have come here? I was curious about his accent and origins; My lifelong obsession with Spirit of Place means I am that way about everyone, as I think places are just as alive as the humans who live there. He had the same quasi-Irish accent that I had, that Geordies in those days developed when far from home and they tried to speak 'proper' English. This was in the years long before they had token Geordies on every telly programme. Many people then just could not catch what was being said. My rival told me was from the north-east

Where?
Newcastle.
Where exactly?
Well not Newcastle itself but a place to north of it.
What place?
Ashington.
Bloody hell! What school?
Ashington Grammar.
What's your name?
Arthur Tennick
Bloodier Hell!

I thought he was vaguely familiar! He had been in the year above me and so didn't know that I even existed. Yet I used to copy - or rather adopt - his very springy step and thought he was what they would now term pretty 'cool'.

Well I was appointed that day as Master i/c of Woodwork and Craft. Although I knew absolutely bugger all about either my powerful implications that I did got me the job. So I gave Arthur a lift back into Bath, not sure whether I should celebrate or not.

En route the conversation took an unusual twist, probably as closet gay people had to do in those days to put out feelers. As I dropped him at

Bath Station he took a deep breath and took out of his briefcase and asked me if I'd ever read this book: *The Mystical Qabalah* by Dion Fortune. With a kind of ta dah! I took out of my briefcase my small *Introduction to the Mystical Qabalah.*

As we would later find out, there were astonishing parallels between us: he was deeply into astrology and had a passion for Cathars (the school was only a couple of miles, as the crow flies from Arthur Guirdham's home); my wife was Chinese, his partner Afro-Caribbean (mixed race partnerships were still rare in those days); I lived in a posh crescent, he lived in a posh crescent. We could have passed as twins – though I feel I was slightly handsomer. On and on, on and on. You get the drift.

The point to my whole yarn being:

If Arthur had got the job that day, it would have been he who wrote *Priestess.*

And this would have been something to do with the energies flowing through both of us from the plateau I call Winsley Hill.

*

As ever, I wrote to a lot of magicians in that period, including Christine Hartley whose book *A Case for Reincarnation* gave numerous anecdotes about this adept known as FPD. Celia and I went to visit her in her wonderful old home in the village of Exton, Hampshire.

Dion, in her *Psychic Self Defence,* described her own (un-named) teacher Theodore

Moriarty as 'An Adept if ever there was one.' Christine was every bit his equal.

I soaked up everything she could tell me about both DNF and FPD but I had no impulse to write about them. I didn't think little me would be up to such a task. That was for the Big People.

Celia and I moved back to the US and settled for a time in Morgantown, West Virginia before our marriage inevitably broke up. I came back to the only place I felt that I belonged - Bath - and started again with a few quid in my bank account and the offer of a job as a nursing assistant in a large home for adults with what was still officially called Mental and Physical Handicaps in a large ex-hospital that was called the Winsley Centre which was a few hundred yards along the valley from Sutcliffe School. I only knew of the place because, during my time at Rock Hall House, we had gone there on an afternoon to liaise.

The unseen chain of association goes thus: if I hadn't falled in love with Dion Fortune I would never have heard of William G. Gray; If I'd never been enthralled by Gray I would never have gone to be near him at Gloucester; if I had never gone to Gloucester I would never have escaped to Bath for my sanity; if I had never gone to Bath I would never have got the job at Rock Hall House; if I hadn't got that job, I would never have known of the Winsley Centre; if I hadn't gone there and met Michelle I would never have moved to the enchanted hamlet of Murhill (just below Winsley) in the Limpley Stoke Valley; and if I'd never been touched by the spirit of the Limpley Stoke Valley I would never have stumbled upon Violet's parents and grandparents, or come to write the sort of books I did - and do!

Phew... I hope you're still with me in all this.

So it was there at the Winsley Centre that I met my second wife Michelle (the mother of my four daughters). And before going out with her, even, the young woman called Margaret who became my third wife. Another long story, but exquisitely relevant to my own quest for Dion Fortune.

Wake up at the back there!

*

It was when Michelle I moved to a rented, haunted house at the bottom of Whitehill in the nearby town of Bradford on Avon that I rebuilt my magical life by contacting again William Gray, Christine Hartley and a host of others including the endlessly sexy and wonderful mage Dolores Ashcroft-Nowicki - the last of the great all-rounders as I saw her, and ex-SIL.

It was now that Christine, perhaps knowing that I had crossed some sort of personal Abyss if not an esoteric one, sent me the Magical Diaries of the workings she did within the Fraternity of the Inner Light, as it was then called, and also next door to it with Kim Seymour.

I told something of this time in the Afterward to the first edition of Priestess, but the essence is as follows...

I can only say the act of transcribing the Diaries from Seymour's hand-written sheets in particular, caused me to go into near-trance states. The inner contacts they worked with such as Lord E., Ne Nefer Ka Ptah and especially the the legendary Kha'm Uast - historically the High Priest of Ptah from Memphis - all these and more seemed to hover around me as I plonked away on the manual typewriter. When I wrote up those rites that involved DNF and the Fraternity of the Inner Light itself, I felt that I was part of the rites. Or at very least peering through into them like Dion did through the mirror at Glastonbury.

I wrote to the SIL and told them what I was doing but they - John Makin again - showed no inclination to help.

I remembered reading Carl Jung's description of the time when his house filled with spirits, resulting in what he called the "spiritual dictation" of his *Seven Sermons to the Dead.*

The pressure within the house was just as intense and we had endless water disasters. The house was already haunted - but dealt with by Dolores - and I am certain in those days that Dion herself came to visit, so to speak.

Michelle, who was a lot younger than me and with no experience of such matters, confessed to me one evening that someone was coming to her during the hours of sleep and whispering in her ear.

She was pregnant; I had to protect her! Then one night, in the wee small hours, although a rotten psychic, I saw the first and only manifestation of this Dion Fortune who had so manipulated my life. I took a deep breath and tried to use a simple banishing technique against her before she got to Michelle. The wraith paused, came around to me side of the bed and, affectionately I thought, slapped me quite tangibly across the face.

*

Aquarian Press gave me an advance of £125 and published these diaries under the title *Dancers to the Gods*. The first chapter, specifically about  Dion Fortune, contained a lot of mistakes and speculations that were just wrong. But I was still doing a full-time job at the Winsley Centre and just could not afford the research needed in those pre-internet days. I did do that thing with my sphincter and asked Dion to help me out so I could buy the birth/marriage/death certificates that were so important and enable me to do proper research at the appropriate libraries, but she sent bugger all my way.

She probably imagined - as did John Makin judging from his snotty comment - that I was likely to earn a large sum of money from the book.

And that's a thing I'd like to get off my little chest... A bit of self-pity (which is the ultimate form of arrogance) coming up here folks. Brace yourselves...

People who don't write imagine that if you get a book published then you must be rolling in money, and that you've also got a room full of your own books just to give away, signed, on asking. When I tell them that my sales per volume can be measured by the dozen rather than the million they think I'm joking. When I tell them that *Priestess* cost me more to research than I ever earned in royalties they again think I'm fibbing. Or else am a mug for even bothering. Over 30-odd years total copies sold of my Dion Fortuney books come to about 6,000.
Personally, I think DNF should be ashamed at neglecting to give fair reward for fair effort. And I don't need to do that thing with my arse to tell her that now.

*

I've got one more stop today and that is back in Trowbridge, at a nursing home a stone's throw from where I live. But I'm having a cuppa at the Lakeside Garden Centre in Crockerton and admiring the little wooden bridge over the water. It makes me think of Penry. Thomas Penry Evans.

Christine Hartley fancied him rotten. She didn't look down upon his common background as some of the others did. She called him Merl as they all did, short for Merlin, testament to his power.

But that wasn't his real Magical Name.

In the days when I was researching him and Violet I stumbled upon a very elderly lady in South Wales called E. Marion Griffiths who gave me a lot of background for that area. My Spirit of Place obsession, see? Although she hadn't met either of them she had been close to Ronald Heaver, who was widely seen as something of a Fisher King character, a guardian of the Holy Grail itself and who used the name Zadok. She knew her stuff, did Marion.

Her scrawled letters were probably written in a pen as fine as mine, and as difficult to read. But she kept asking in each one of the initials BBBB meant anything to me, as she kept getting these letters psychically.

They meant nothing. I wanted to tell her this was astral junk but I was either too cowardly or too polite to do so. Many years later, when she was long gone, I learned from Gareth Knight that Penry's name within the lodge, unknown to any outsiders, was Bid Ben Bid Bont.

You might want to google that and see what it means, and why it was so relevant, and why I'm thinking of it now.

To a lesser degree I had all the synchronicities involving Penry as I had with Violet but it would be tedious to recount all these too.

The tea is okay here but the cakes are overpriced. Yet there's always a stillness that has nothing to do with lack of noise, as I've yarned about before.

And now, dear readers, my last stop of the day where I try very hard not to cry...

This is just down the road from me where – astonishingly – my mother's 90-something year old cousin has been moved by her daughter, from Ashington. As she's the spitting image of my own Mam it's uncanny to talk to her, although she recognises no-one. She remembers and can talk about all the *places*, but none of her family. She can't understand the Tamil accents of the staff, but is grateful to hear me as I get mine back for her. Until she came to the home I had last seen her when I was four.

Her only child Joyce and I were the same age and went through school together although we'd lost contact after we we last acted together in Karel Capek's *Insect Play* at 17.

Even more bizarrely Joyce, unrecognised by me, had been teaching two of my kids for years on Winsley Hill before we twigged .

In some odd way Aunty Jean is a means of me making peace with my own late Mam. She is gentle, she is loving, she has forgotten almost everything. As I kneel before her and kiss her hand the nightmare times and parental Mam-induced violences of Ariel Street fade away. Somehow, I am able to achieve the forgiveness for which I have long striven. She gives me peace. It's not Aunty Jean I'm speaking to when I whisper: *Mam, I loved you.*

You did your best. I know that. I loved you and always will. But I make sure that Jean doesn't hear and get more confused.

Odd, so very odd.

Again, that's all Dion Fortune's fault.

*

With the publication of *Dancers* I felt that my work was over. In magical terms, I was so plugged in to the currents channelled by Seymour and Hartley that I was busy making sense of those energies that would eventually see the light of day as *Earth God Rising* and *The Inner Guide to Egypt*.

As I outlined in the former, Michelle and I and baby Zoe moved into the old gardener's cottage in the grounds of Murhill Manor on the edge of Winsley Hill. A truly enchanted, faery-haunted spot.

I knew that several others were planning to do a full biography of Dion, but I was quite happy to let anyone else use what I'd written and expand on it. It was almost as though DNF had created a simultaneous global short-list of candidates:

There was someone in Australia; someone called A.C. Highfield who complained in a magazine about 'Occult Establishment obstructionism' (I guess he'd been blanked by Makin too); the American fantasy writer Katherine Kurtz; Janine Chapman from Florida,

I think, and someone called Charles Fielding. The latter, I was told, had the financial backing of the Texan millionaire Carr Collins.

Good luck to them all, I thought.

Yet once again I woke - or was woken - in the middle of the night by the certainty that if anyone did this it *had* to be me. It *had* to be a Brit. Not that I was, or am, xenophobic, but a non-Brit might not get the nuances. They wouldn't understand what would make a Yorkshire Lass like Violet Firth the sort of person she was, or appreciate the completely different tone, style and attitudes between different areas in the (to them) small island of Britain.

I know from long experience that Americans, for example, always say that they 'get' the British and their humour, their irony,

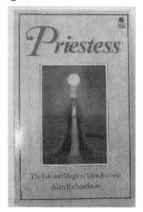

self-deprecation and self-mockery, they really do - but they don't. Not ever. Except perhaps for Bill Bryson.

She had to be done by a Brit.

So Aquarian Press gave me a £250 advance this time and 2% of publisher's profits as royalties (I was told many years later that this was pathetic) and I set to work ordering all the birth/marriage/death certificates and also a couple of wills.

Again I'd like to point out that I was still working full time, as an aide in an Old Peoples' Home in Westbury. I was doing 40 hours a week plus two sleep-ins. We got the one-up and one-down cottage in Murhill for a peppercorn rent but on the proviso that I tended the very large garden. I came to loathe gardening and had dreams of applying Agent Orange all over the estate to lighten my workload.

I bought a small, silent electronic typewriter that used thermal paper so that I could work during my night-shifts, and also not disturb either Michelle or the baby when I was at home. Plus lots of A4 notebooks on which I would write on one side only, using the left page for random ideas and additions to be put together later.

I deliberately started the manuscript of what I originally entitled *Priestess in the Orchard* on December 6th, her birthday.

Using up my publishers' advance I took the bus to Somerset House in London where I could look through all the folders giving references to the birth certificates - though not the documents themselves. You had to take a chance that you got the right one. The dust jacket of *Psychic Self Defence* had said she died in 1946 at the age of 55. Therefore, I assumed she had been born in 1891. I got three other Violet Mary Firths before

I found Our Lady tucked away at the end of 1890.

Once I got that and found her parents names, I was able to go back to Somerset House and saw that Arthur Firth and Sarah Jane Smith had been married in Bradford (West) in 1887. As my advance money was running out rapidly I got my friends Tim and Jenny Owen, who lived in Yorkshire to look through the library records for Bradford on microfiche to see if they could track them down - a joyless, miserable task to which they stuck bravely, without any result.

I knew about the Yorkshire connection because Firth stainless steel was a household name, and Francis King's seminal book *Ritual Magic in England* mentioned her Yorkshire childhood without going into any real detail.

(Actually I stumbled on that book in the Samye-Ling Monastery in the Scottish Borders in 1970. We were on a trip from college. I showed off with my Rampa-imbued knowledge. I pointed out *dorjes* and *katas* and *chortens* and name-dropped *Padmasambhava* as if he'd been a regular in the East End Social Club. The young lama in charge seemed impressed: 'Do you speak Tibetan?' he asked. The other students threw things at me afterwards, in the bus, but I think they were impressed too.)

Finally, Dion must have felt a bit guilty because she nudged someone called Philip Carver (ex-SIL) to give me another £50, and with that I bought the all-important marriage certificate.

When it finally arrived I couldn't quite believe what I read. Her parents didn't get married some 300 miles away in the western part of the Yorkshire city of Bradford as I assumed. They got married in the Church of St Mary the Virgin, in the village of Limpley Stoke, in the registration district of Bradford on Avon in the West Country.

That is, at the other end of the valley in which we were living. In a church I had passed many times and always vowed to enter one day, as it seemed as if it might hold secrets. It did.

Her grandparents were so much in love with the place they were buried there, next to the pagan holy spot, with 13 Templar graves almost guarding them.

They lived at and ran the Limpley Stoke Hydropathic Establishment, which - as a simple hotel - I'd used as something of a local for many years.

The bearded patriarch above is John Smith, her adored grandfather. It is quite likely that her grandmother, mother and father are in this grouping. As ever with these things, I stumbled upon this photo completely unexpectedly.

Should I put a signpost on my time-line here or a monolith? As I wrote, somewhat portentously in the second Thoth Publications edition of *Priestess* (the one that pays no royalties):

> So, when Arthur Firth came down from the solar centre of Sheffield with all its fire and steel, to stay at a spa hotel in a small village in a lost valley in the West Country, then without knowing it he had brought Lord Sun and Lady Moon together in a rite that revolves without end.

I think it's true. Certainly for me personally. If things related to Dion Fortune has always surged into my life before this, I was now under a tsunami. I suppose I should have expected this from a Sea Priestess.

The Library Angel worked overtime. Often I was compelled to go to the little library at Bradford on Avon, just a couple of miles down the valley, and I'd find just the obscure book I was looking for. Sometimes they were even displayed as if waiting for me.

Old copies of Kelly's Directory (a sort of early Yellow Pages-cum-telephone directory) flew at me and enabled me to identify or locate the long-lost individuals or businesses I was interested in.

Complete strangers made contact, more than happy to look up things in distant libraries or town records.

I managed to connect with the last survivors of Dion's era before they passed away, and gleaned what I needed from them. I cannot now remember how I became aware of Eleanor Whittall but from her I learned exactly where the occult college hidden in the 'sandy fastness of the Hampshire Barrens' had been - because she had attended when young Violet was there! And couldn't stand her.

It turned out that Sir Vincent and Lady Caillard from whom Mrs Evans bought the Belfry and turned it into a Temple of Isis had lived just down the road also, on the edge of Trowbridge.

Mystics passed on messages from her - but they were always wrong. I had vivid dreams in which Dion gave me the details I was trying to find - and they were always wrong too.

That's just a brief summary. Believe me it was unrelenting, infinitely varied. Exhausting and thrilling.

*

It's my lunch-break and I'm typing this in the back of the Van. I've taken the little-known high road over from Pewsey, across the hills and down toward the garrison town of Tidworth, widely known as the armpit of Wiltshire. I stop on a high place and keep my engine running while guzzling a roll of multi-grain seeded bread containing sliced turkey breast with home-made cranberry sauce and various green things that Margaret made for me. She spoils me rotten. Today I will even try to drive straight past the excellent truck stop that normally exerts a Circean call.

It was a couple of years ago, I think (time gets elastic for me these days) , that I had an inexplicable experience on this route in my Van. After enormous inner pressure I had finally finished the manuscript of my dual-biography *Aleister Crowley and Dion Fortune - Logos of the Aeon, Shakti of the Age.*[1] When it 'came through' in the middle of night I knew that I had to write it in a mad way: from their deaths, backward to their birth and before. By looking at them this wise I saw parallels that had hitherto eluded me. It was a strange and disturbing experience to tell their tales in a one-step forward and two-steps back sort of way.

Yet as I headed back home to Trowbridge, filled with a kind of after-thrumming of the

---

[1] LLewellyn, USA.

whole process, I suddenly found myself in a place I should not (could not) have been, miles from where I **should** have been, completely disoriented and confused.

That's the essence of a complex story that would take too long to describe here and for which I have no explanation. Almost as though AC and DF got together and said: *Let's show the little sod what we can do.*

I had a similar episode when I was deep in the throes of writing *Priestess.*

While on my way to meet Michelle in Milsom Street, in Bath, it was almost as though a

schoolmaster-entity grabbed me by the lug-hole and almost frog-marched me to the old Reference Library in Queen's Square. I felt myself half-flung into the Local Studies corner where I was immediately drawn to a slim book about Sexey's School in Somerset. There, front left of the photograph of a school trip to Brean

Down, was Violet Firth. I just knew it was her, and someone confirmed this much later.

So perhaps you can see that in those days I managed to put together, piece by piece, a picture of Violet Firth's world, rather than that of Dion Fortune. Not complete by any means, though. I don't imagine she gave a damn about Little Alan as such, but I do think she wanted at least someone give her family a plug.

By now I came to understand something of the Mysteries behind the plateau I know as Winsley Hill, around which the Limpley Stoke Valley curves. I wrote this up in the last edition of *Priestess* but I think it's important to have a cut-and-paste of the whole section here because this is the story behind Violet Firth's parents and also behind me.

*

"The whole of that Limpley Stoke valley and the Winsley plateau which forms one side of its curve are soaked in Earth Mysteries both ancient and modern, as it seems to have drawn people there over the millennia, all linked by the same themes. There are standing stones, fragmented avenues and near-forgotten stone circles scattered across the fields.

"Guy Underwood, who is some ways is a Founding Father of dowsing, did his first researches there. Arthur Guirdham whose books on the Cathars and group reincarnation had such impact on the 'New Age' had his visions and wrote his books in nearby Bathford.

"Clinging to the hillside further along from Limpley Stoke is the hamlet of Conkwell with its holy well known as the Spring of the Green Man, and just beyond that is the locale known anciently as No Man's Land, which hints at Women's Mysteries once worked where the old circle and the three roads meet. William Smith the 'Father of English Geology' who formulated the stratification of the soil and rocks lived in nearby Tucking Mill.

"While Chris Patton, Britain's very first 'Green Minister' responsible for Environmental Affairs was given his appointment when living on the hilltop overlooking that holy valley.

"And Terence Meaden who did so much early research into Crop Circles and the faces in the Avebury Goddess Stones lived and worked in Bradford on Avon at the mouth of the valley.

"As far as churches go the only Catholic Church in that immediate area is dedicated to St Thomas More.

"In Winsley village St Nicholas – often linked with the old fertility gods – has a church dedicated to him which was built on the site a huge dolmen, overlooking the valley.

"While in the other direction, very close by, the Church of St Mary the Virgin lies on a side road which leads down from the busy A36, sloping and winding toward the plush and trim village of Freshford. Hidden by hedgerow and dry-stone wall it can easily be missed by the motorist. In all the centuries it has not changed much. Long before Christ, long before the Romans, longer still before the Druids, this had been a holy place Even now the actual site of the original pagan worship still survives within the church grounds, although it is marked by no more than a curvature of the wall. Legend has it that the original builders tried to put the church lower down the valley, but that the Devil himself made them put it where it now stands. From that unexceptional curve in the wall the land beyond drops steeply though not dramatically. The eye is made to fly like a witch over the curvature of fields towards Westwood.

"Once, a young and fertile goddess was worshipped here, nubile but sightless, ever-giving but ever-chaste. By the time the Christians came the goddess was changed to St Mary the Virgin.

"Even the early Fathers understood something of the true nature of virginity, which meant not so much an intact hymen as a consideration of being *one-in-herself*, as only a goddess can be.[1] This way, female deities of the fields and the corn were to be transmuted into the Virgin Mary, who according to the system of the magicians, was also Isis, and Keridwen, and Fiân - Herne's own lady - queen of the valley

---

[1] see *Women's Mysteries* by M. Esther Harding for a discussion of the paradox whereby the Cosmic Whore and Eternal Virgin are one and the same.

and streams. Although the colours might change a little, all else remains always the same.

"Within the churchyard itself are the tombs of thirteen Anglo-Norman nobles, Templars everyone of them. Sometimes, sitting very still, so quiet that the other senses can come out as delicate as mice, they can still be sensed: brooding but not hostile, autocratic but not cruel. They were men whose lands became rich on wool as their newish and nominal lord, Jesus, became mighty through the formula of the Lamb, and can still surge with recognition at the old Latin of *Pax Vobiscum*, said softly above their stones.

"This is the church where Dion Fortune's parents married, where her grandparents' graves can still be seen, and where young Violet's echo has also been noted."

*

Well, a bit OTT in retrospect, but you get the idea.

*

It seemed to me that her parents Arthur and Jenny, as she preferred to be called, who met, courted and married in the Limpley Stoke and Winsley Hill environs, picked up something of the Earth Magic of the place. Or if not her parents, certainly her beloved maternal grandparents, John and Elizabeth Smith, who were buried there.

Although the latter were what we would now think of as New Agey types with a passion for Alternative Medicine and 19th Century state-of-the-art Health Spas, I doubt if they would have had any conscious awareness of this small area in the terms I have just described. But I think they were infected by a kind of spiritual 'tone', and inner song very like that which you can discern in the novel *The Sea Priestess*. And they passed this on to young Violet when she arrived, a couple of years later.

I had experience of this inner tone myself, when I was compelled to write my novella *On Winsley Hill*[1]. No matter how much I tried to alter the style, I couldn't. It was as though I was taken over by *something* that was determined to get a song across, and express itself through my prose. Try as I might, I couldn't change the style, and haven't been able to emulate it since.

 Was this Dion Fortune speaking through me? No, probably not. But I do think it was an impulse from the hill itself – an impulse that may well have been passed down to young

[1] Skylight Press 2011. That's the Sun Disk central to the story.

Violet via her family.

Well, that's the best that I can explain it.

*

I suppose that I've just about covered the main impulses which flowed through me when writing *Priestess*. There are many others, as I think I've said, but I have a life-long horror of sounding boring so please fill these out with your own yarns.

Even after the book was published there were curious echoes from Dion Fortune - almost as if she was having some fun with me.

Once, in the mid 80s I got a summons from the tax man asking me to explain why, in over 15 years, I had never paid any tax on my *Introduction to the Mystical Qabalah*. This was signed by Mr W.N. Fortune. I had to pay HM government a total of £200 back tax. I think Mr Fortune was bemused by the synchronicity. We were so broke they allowed me to pay by instalments.

Y'see before I started writing *Priestess* I did that thing with my sphincter again and made an agreement up in the air with Dion that I would pay 10% of anything I earned from writing about her to the charity Cancer and Leukaemia in Childhood, known by the acronym of CLIC. When my third and final lot of royalties came I dutifully wrote out a cheque for, as I recall, £27.00 but left it in an envelope addressed to the charity on the side of our fridge. I had to wait until I got paid from my full time job or else it would have bounced. In due course I then gave the envelope to my second daughter Kirsty, who was only 4, and stood at the door and watched as she toddled over to the post-box.

As soon as she got back the phone rang. It was a neighbour at the end of our street screaming down the phone at me: "Alan hang up and look above your house - LOOK ABOVE YOUR HOUSE!"

I poked my head out and looked up, and there about 20 feet above our chimney was the huge hot-air balloon with the CLIC logo bulging out. Inside the basket were two people, a man and a woman. They waved down at me as the balloon slowly rose again.

I knew the charity itself was based in Yeovil, half a world away from Winsley Hill. The odds against it appearing, there and then...?

I sat on my doorstep and smiled and watched them go. I knew that in a sense this was Violet and Penry waving goodbye to me. My job was done.

Then there was a time recently when my wife and I went to the wedding of one of her friends in Brussels. The males there were all old school friends of the groom, Michael. No-one else knew each other and Michael had neither met me nor knew anything about me.

On our table at the reception to my left was a delightful man who had also been a teenage member of the Air Training Corps. We had delicious conversation about the merits of the Hurricane v Spitfire, the futuristic design of the Messerschmitt 262 and jointly lamented the cancellation of the fighter-bomber known as the TSR 2 by the government at the time. Margaret, needless to say was glassy-eyed by all this.

Then I got talking to the man on my right, a Mr Dyson, who – among others things - confessed quite shyly that he had just written a book.

What about?

About Mrs Wyatt Earp. Called 'Meet the Wife'.

I was all ears. I like cowboys, and have been called a cowboy myself many times, in my various jobs. Especially by the lads in the loading bay

When is it due out?

Well, it should have been last week but the publishers had to cancel.

Why?

Well, there are no known photographs of Mrs Earp so I plucked a photo from the internet of some old boiler whom I thought fitted Mrs Earp's style and used that as the cover. But at the last moment one of the editors turned up in a panic and said that I couldn't use that, as it was a photo of an apparently well-known woman called 'Dion Fortune' – whoever she was. Well, honestly, have YOU ever heard of this 'Dion Fortune'?

Then there are the numerous women I have met who earnestly believed that they are Dion reborn. None of them were cranky. They lived decent lives, doing proper jobs, had normal relationships in what is often called the 'real' world. William Gray (who had known DNF on the outer and inner planes) once told me that a particular lady 'was DF reborn!' Later on, when their relationship decayed as they did with most people in Gray's odd life, he decided that he had got that wrong. Later on, she too decided it was more a case of her being overshadowed than reincarnation as such.

Well we all make complete idiots of ourselves at various points along the Path, and as a young lad I had wonderful times as Vlad the Impaler, Napoleon III, Grigoriyevich Rasputin and D.H. Lawrence. The only danger is when you expect everyone else to believe this, and fail to accept within your own self that – almost certainly – something else is going on.

These days I'm more inclined to think in terms of Other Lives than past lives. That is, time is not linear. Everything is happening now, at this instant, ever-becoming.

I suppose in connection with this I did have one bit of personal channelling that came to me one night which I felt was inspired by DNF. I called it the *Microcosmic Doctrine*

> All magic is essentially tribal. This tribe can best be visualised as a circle (or even a sphere). Half of it is in the Otherworld, half in the Earthworld. It is a circle which links past, present and future and makes no distinction. The tribe contains souls which are incarnate, souls between lives, souls which have ceased incarnation, plus beings which have never been and never will be incarnate.
>
> Each tribe has a succession of leaders in the Earthworld. Their job is to bring through the Magical Current. In their turn they are overshadowed by tribal leaders from the Otherworld - what are termed the 'Secret Chiefs.' In fact, if we can, think of that as being in the sense 'Chief of the Clan McDonald,' or 'Chief of the Clan McGregor.' The tone and the style of the tribe alters according to which Chief and

which Earthworld priest or priestess is predominant at the time. The tribe might grow, change, or contract, but the centre will remain the same.

When a newcomer links with the tribe he can tap the collective wisdom of the tribal mind. Often when this happens he has visions of what may appear to be past lives but which are more nearly tribal visions, or points of collective experience down through the ages. These are not always to be taken personally.

Sometimes the newcomer will feel him/herself overshadowed by a tribal member from the Otherworld. A mistake can be made here by believing him/herself to be an actual incarnation of that entity.

Tribes can, do, and should overlap. The Chiefs and the Earthworld leaders come and go, but their essence remains within the tribe. The Chiefs, therefore, are not meant to be worshipped, for they are points of contact between the worlds. They are part of us as we are part of them. Each member of the tribe is part of one corporate whole. We cannot worship them for we would be worshipping ourselves.

Whatever intellectual output might result is less important than the personal sense of contact with the Otherworld, and linkage with the collective consciousness of the tribe.

When I first researching *Priestess* I discovered an awful lot of people who felt they had meaningful links with her. In fact I doubt if there is any DNF ' fan' out there was doesn't have some link. To anyone else, they might seem feeble, but to the person in question, they are keys.

One man's grandparent had gone to the same school as Violet's father. Another woman's grandparents had worked in the Firth stainless steel manufacturing complexes in Sheffield. Another, whose husband is well known in the magical fields, went to the same school as young Violet but a couple of generations later. They were connections usually based upon place, time or sometimes just odd but meaningful parallels in their lives. Or else they felt that her books seemed to be speaking to them personally. Plus many, many more.

I think we all like to feel ourselves connected with someone who is global – however remote the celebrity might be from the reality of their lives. Hence the spiritualists (and I'm not knocking them and never will) who link with Elvis, or Michael Jackson or Thomas More. I heard second and third hand of an individual who claimed to be Violet's illegitimate child. She was quite happy to have this cachet in the small esoteric circles in which she moved; I tried to contact her but was unsuccessful. Yet, if she had been Violet's child, and she really wanted to be acknowledged as such within her group, then at that time the best person to confirm this was... me. She has passed away now, I think.

Given the storm of material that was flung my way, I briefly wondered if *I* was DF reborn. But I can tell you with complete certainty that this was never the case.

I think that if there is any sort of 'answer' to such an unanswerable mystery, it might be to do with the Overself, or what the Egyptians termed the Ba – a concept I grasp a lot better than the former. Kim Seymour had the best insight even then, when he wrote in that essay I first read as a fevered teen:

> This Individuality or Genius in its turn sends forth from itself a portion of its own substance which is called the Lower Self, and this latter is that natural phenomenon which is known during earth life as Mr. Jones or Miss Smith. And let it be said (you can disagree if you like for no proof is possible) that as Mr. Jones and Miss Smith you incarnate. But Mr. Jones and Miss Smith only *incarnate*. They never reincarnate. It is the *Higher Self* of each one of us that seeks reincarnation by incarnating a little bit at a time. And the non-incarnating portion of Mr. Jones and Miss Smith is the Observer, the Guardian at the Gate, etc.

To be honest I don't fully grasp that very last sentence, but I'll keep working at it.

*

All of which just goes to say that 'my' Dion Fortune became an essential part of my own inner bias toward this Spirit of Place thingy that has bothered me, battered me sometimes, but by and large inspired me for most of my life. I've never fully understood everything that has gone on between me and her, but I'm adamant that you've all got your own stories to tell, and your own bewilderments to express. Nobody is ahead of anyone else in this respect, neither better nor wiser.

The Gnostics, as you know, had a single Big Idea, and it was simply expressed as: *All is One*. That's all. Three short words that are wonderful in their simplicity, yet infinite in their depth. And as Arthur Guirdham once wrote from his study at the far edge of the Winsley plateau: "We Are One Another." We can all can link our Dion Fortune stories with marvellous equality.

The one thing I can be dogmatic about, is that no-one can be dogmatic about Dion Fortune. Whether *she* is a great soul on the inner planes, or *it* is a flow of energy rather like an electrical current, shouldn't worry us too much.

*

It's Saturday today. I'm scribbling this on the terrace of the Limpley Stoke Hotel waiting to meet two friends of ours who live in a house built on land once owned or managed by the Smiths and Firths. David has been getting the

Inner Light magazine for very many years now although he doesn't know why. He did apply to join the SIL many many years ago but was turned down because he is gay.

We have just come from the church in Limpley Stoke where I said hello to the Smiths, and told the Templars: *Pax Vobiscum.* This is one of our holy places and sometimes we go inside and say the Paternoster. I am not a Catholic, I have to say, and neither is Margaret but I keep a copy of the Latin Lord's Prayer in my wallet and read it out loud in places like this. Sometimes they sort of perk up as the old stones hear the Old Tongue spoken once more.

I like all the hotels in our area. It is possible to get a large pot of tea and biscuits for under a fiver which will provide me with around five cups in comfortable surroundings. Compare this to the service stations on the motorway in which you pay nearly three quid for some boiling water in a plastic cup with a tea bag and a plastic stirrer. Lots of other hotels have gone under but somehow the Limpley Stoke Hotel survives, specialising in weddings and the occasional conference.

Margaret drinks her Gin and Slimline Tonic and browses the local paper, the *Wiltshire Times.*

Keeping the best biscuits well out of her reach I gaze at the older corner of the hotel near where we sit, which is a part that Arthur and Jenny would still recognise. I am sure they stole a kiss or two there, before going public. I have a sense of them occasionally; they are so much younger than I am now. A handsome couple. I think that's probably all that Dion wanted from me, to acknowledge them in a human way.

We've got a week of annual leave stretching ahead of us and we're off to West Wales to savour the delights of the stunning Gower Peninsular and Pembrokeshire coast. If I never felt any kind of emotional attachment to the Somerset Levels and the Avalonian dreamlands around Glastonbury that were so important to Our Violet, then perhaps I'm becoming enraptured by Penry's secret landscapes.

Have I finished this book now? I think of what I've written so far.

It's a curious and sometimes uncomfortable thing, sinking back into the astral form of the lanky, gawky boy I was. Although I was useless at football and dreaded double Games, I did still daydream of one day being a tricky winger or midfield maestro for Newcastle United. Or else a steely-eyed jet fighter in the RAF, wracked by g-forces but blasting Migs out of the skies above Ashington in my supersonic English Electric Lightning with Firestreak missiles.

Yet although my true, deepest passion was for the Magic of Dion Fortune and her ilk, never once did I have serious dreams of joining her lodge – or any lodge - and working to become the best Magus in the Temple. Nor did I ever want to join William G. Gray's group – or any group - when I lived near him, although the offer was there. It must seem absurd but the only real daydream I had with respect to the SIL at that time was that I might one day pop around for tea and cakes, and be made welcome, and have them listen to my yarns.

In fact a couple of years ago, after *Aleister Crowley and Dion Fortune* came out, of which (to my astonishment) they seemed to approve, I got exactly that invite. Although I was about to have a hefty and serious operation the next day and had fears of my own imminent demise, they were charming, they were kind and supportive, and the tea and cakes were sublime. I am not sure if the feeling was mutual, or if I'm projecting too much, but when I entered 38 Steele's Road I felt that I'd come home, after a long, long walk from Woodhorn Road in Ashington.

I mentioned earlier about the Being who advised someone: *Find a King and ask for gold.*

As I sit here in an area that makes me sing, knowing that I have four grown-up beautiful daughters who not only love me as a Dad but also seem to like me as Alan, three enchanting grandchildren who regularly exclaim *Grandad Alan is sooooo silly, isn't he?* and my beautiful, fey, brilliant wife Margaret whom the rest of them also adore, I suppose that with respect to Dion I found myself a Queen, asked for gold, and was given the real stuff in abundance.

Yes, yes indeed, we are one another folks. All are One. All is one.

And you're welcome to come on board my magical Van and join the Wiltshire Library Service any place you can track me down...

I Remember, I Remember

I remember, I remember,
The house where I was born,
The little window where the sun
Came peeping in at morn;
He never came a wink too soon,
Nor brought too long a day,
But now, I often wish the night
Had borne my breath away!

I remember, I remember,
The roses, red and white,
The vi'lets, and the lily-cups,
Those flowers made of light!
The lilacs where the robin built,
And where my brother set
The laburnum on his birthday,—
The tree is living yet!

I remember, I remember,
Where I was used to swing,
And thought the air must rush as fresh
To swallows on the wing;
My spirit flew in feathers then,
That is so heavy now,
And summer pools could hardly cool
The fever on my brow!

I remember, I remember,
The fir trees dark and high;

I used to think their slender tops
Were close against the sky:
It was a childish ignorance,
But now 'tis little joy
To know I'm farther off from heav'n
Than when I was a boy.

Appendix 2

(from the Afterward to *Sex and Light* aka *The Google Tantra)*

Call me Walter, Prince of Softies if you like, but when I finished the original typescript of *The Google Tantra – How I became the First Geordie to Raise the Kundalini,* I thought that The Maxwell should have a chance to read my take on him.

We had been friends from about the age of 14 and during those inwardly formative years I had babbled and burbled incessantly about this new realm of 'The Occult' that so obsessed me, without him once showing the slightest interest in anything more exalted than porn, booze, cigarettes, Newcastle United and girls – though not necessarily in that order.

Maxwell as Sex God
c.1971

Many years later I would have possible 'far memories' of him having done me to death along the Roman Wall when I had been a young Roman officer involved in the cult of Mithras, and him a wild, tattooed and very angry Pict. But in this life, in our Ashingtonian teens, I was clearly more spiritually advanced than him.

After all, I rarely swore, was far less libidinous as befitted my refined nature, didn't drink or smoke until much later on and then only in moderation, and had never had a fight in my life; whereas he seemed to be permanently at war with most of his peers and was once proclaimed as being the Hardest Lad in Ashington at the age of 12.

Honestly, he was a club-wielding Neanderthal to my fire-making Cro-Magnon. A brutish Mr Hyde to my urbane Doctor Jekyll. He was a Creature from the Abyss while I was obviously one of the glittering, soaring Seraphim – especially as far as my Mam was concerned. Although he was from the posh houses on Maple Street where they had indoor toilets, baths and hot running water, how could an *untermensch* like him, possibly understand about such things as kundalinis, eh?

So I found his letter rather illuminating…

Richardson you git…

Did I ever tell you of my own mystical experiences? It must have been back in late '69 or early '70 because there was a covering of snow everywhere. I was with Queenie at the time and we were strolling across Peoples Park. I cannot remember where we had been (perhaps the Portland) but it was about 9 pm. Suddenly the serpent stirred deep in my loins and I suddenly had a desperate need to get my end away. Not the most promising spot in Ashington you may think considering the weather but I was nothing if not resourceful.

Those were the days of mini-skirts, hot pants and maxi-coats. Queenie's coat was down to her ankles and quite thick (this probably made it knee length on non dwarfs). I quickly found a bench which still had the correct number of planks and brushed some of the snow off it. Excitedly I pulled off her little hot pants and being a gentleman gave her to use them as a pillow — couldn't let her get a cold head could I? Not gentleman John. Knickers were swiftly removed and put in my duffel coat pocket so they wouldn't get wet or too cold, loons were dropped to knee level and I was away like a rabbit on speed. Unfortunately this coat of Queenie's had a split up the back to facilitate walking. The thrusting and gyrating, combined with the icy planks of the bench, made it open up and nearing the orgasmic thrust, my bollocks ploughed between the pleat and into the ice below.

I remember the sharp intake of breath, the fire ascending through my spine, my head exploding and then standing among the stars. I cannot really say how long I was in this state of communion with the cosmos but I recall being drawn back into my body and hearing the words

"Fucking Hell" ringing in my ears. It didn't sound like Queenie so I suppose the utterance had come from my own lips. "Oooh John", was her reaction. Bollocks suddenly shrinking to the size of acorns and emptying their contents in one seismic contraction certainly produced a copious ejaculation. Strangely enough my dick seemed to get bigger — must have been the extra blood diverted from the scrotal area. To get out of the ice I arched and thrust harder than ever before which must have caused extra clitoral stimulation as she then had her own little Cuntaleenie experience (Honolulu tantric term that is.) This certainly seems to parallel some of the things you seek in your book — if only you had asked. (It was even better than the knee trembler we had against the main doors of the Grand Hotel, 1 am, New Years morning, 1970.)

Later that year I had another serpent experience. Queenie couldn't get the pill on a regular basis so we had to resort to coitus interruptus or rubber. Neither were satisfactory so she got some spermicidal tablets off her Aunt Edith (Eedie). They were white and about an inch in diameter. One was placed in the vagina prior to intercourse where it foamed up to provide a sperm killing zone. After the initial foreplay to get the necessary damp conditions needed for activation, the tablet was inserted. Once again we were off like demented bunnies. All was well for about two minutes and then I started to feel my bell end burning. At first I thought it might be a stray pube acting like a cheese cutter but the sensation worsened and I was forced to withdraw. By this time she was also experiencing a burning sensation. A mad dash to the bathroom followed tits and bollocks flailing about madly. She went straight for the bath and I for the sink.

My relief came quicker than hers as it takes less time to fill a sink with cold water and plunge your dick into it than it does to fill a bath and try to get water into an orifice not designed for this purpose. Again the serpent flew up my spine and exploded though the top of my head as the cold water doused the flames which had ignited on my now very red prick. It was a week before we could resume screwing but after two days the one eyed snake shed the skin covering its head. Does this have a mystical significance?

It was shortly after this that we went to college and I split with Queenie. I had many other wondrous experiences there, but for the present they shall remain undisclosed.

If you wish to use any of this trivia you are more than welcome.

By the way, you did not mention that you were considered the 'Ideal Lad' by my mother. She always was gullible and credulous as hell. Mind, she always thought [Apollo] Fuge was a tit when he tried the same ploys as you. Remember calling for me when you knew I wouldn't be in and saying to her, "I'm just going to get my hair cut and was wondering if John wanted to come as well?" Lying bastard. By the way what's a fucking semi-colon? I must have been off the day they taught us that. I know it's not part of the digestive tract.

Your ever willing foil, (or fool) Maxwell

Remember that famous phrase? 'Be careful how you speak to the beggar you meet in the road: it might be the Buddha.'

In the light of his letter we might modify this to read: 'Be careful about dismissing the foul-mouthed fella singing bad Karaoke at the end of the bar as someone who couldn't possibly understand high esoteric things: it might be The Maxwell.'

Which goes to prove my point: you don't need to go looking for professional gurus or be impressed by their robes, soft voices, noble sentiments and apparent attainment. There are people around you in your everyday life, who, without any publicity or thought of gain, without being members of any group or cult, and showing no obvious signs of having any deep philosophies or being 'spiritual' persons at all, are having inner experiences that are astonishing, profound, and really quite awesome. They are the real teachers.

So thanks to that letter I now have to give my old pal The Maxwell his due and go back in time to recast the original manuscript with a slightly revised title: *The Google Tantra – How I became the **Second** Geordie to Raise the Kundalini.*

What a sod, eh? He's ruined my fuckin' book. I should never have let him copy my homework.

Made in the USA
Las Vegas, NV
24 September 2023

78044461R00059